The Gordons of Tallahassee

LaVerne Gordon Goodridge

with

Sarah Gordon Weathersby

ISBN: 978-0-6151-9689-3

Printed in the United States of America.

FOREWORD

Family stories are easily lost, especially in these times when children leave home and move far and wide from the place where it all began. Family reunions are times when the old stories may be repeated, but the young ones often don't listen. Some stories are never retold because of embarrassment or feelings of shame, and the failure to recognize that regardless of how dour our circumstances may have been, that was where we came from. Even our mixed heritage should be a source of our strength.

My siblings and I often heard the stories of our grandmother, Mattie. My sister LaVerne, as the oldest had the foresight to write down the story as told by our Mother before she died in 1958. LaVerne gave us all a typed copy that in my case was read and filed in a drawer of assorted family documents.

LaVerne went further in writing her own story of growing up as the first child of Robert and Georgia Gordon. She worked on it nearly fifty years as she remembered bits and pieces of all the places they lived and the churches Daddy served in his ministry through Georgia, Florida, West Virginia, and Virginia.

As the years passed, LaVerne developed decreasing patience with her computer, and declining memory of the names of people and places, until I took it upon myself to intervene. I hijacked her manuscript with the intention of crafting it into a story to be passed on to our progeny.

I found, however, the story needed no crafting, but it was missing the ending; I hadn't been born yet. I called on my brothers to fill in the gaps to get us to Petersburg where I was born. Their tales of growing up as four brothers who followed their big sister, tales of adventure and mischief, were their story, not LaVerne's. I wanted to keep LaVerne's voice. No one else could have told of the "halcyon period" of our parents. No one else could express Mother's motives for marrying "that yellow man."

And so begins the Saga of the Gordons of Tallahassee.

S.I.N.

Hamilton-Gordon Family

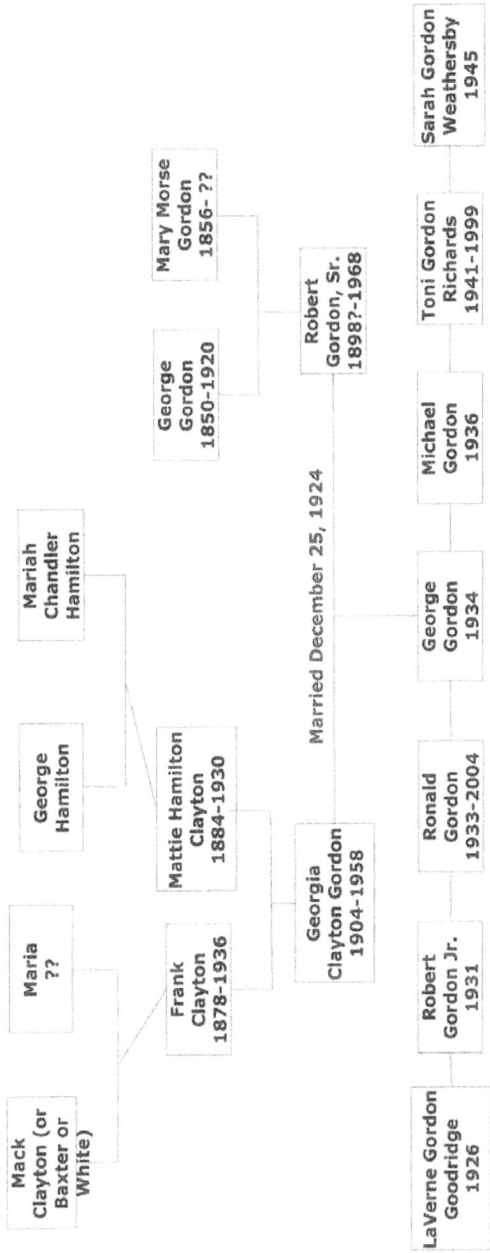

Mack Clayton (or Baxter or White)

Maria ??

George Hamilton

Mariah Chandler Hamilton

George Gordon 1850-1920

Mary Morse Gordon 1856- ??

Frank Clayton 1878-1936

Mattie Hamilton Clayton 1884-1930

Robert Gordon, Sr. 1898?-1968

Georgia Clayton Gordon 1904-1958

Married December 25, 1924

LaVerne Gordon Goodridge 1926

Robert Gordon Jr. 1931

Ronald Gordon 1933-2004

George Gordon 1934

Michael Gordon 1936

Toni Gordon Richards 1941-1999

Sarah Gordon Weathersby 1945

S.G.W

The Gordons of Tallahassee

Georgia's Story

The Gordons of Tallahassee

Crying Holy unto the Lord,
Crying Holy unto the Lord,
I've been introduced to the Father and the Son
And I ain't no stranger now.

A plaintive voice rose from the packed gallery. It began as a barely audible hum. It gradually rose and finally broke loose spilling as a flood unleashing all of the broken dreams, and sorrows, and despair, and lost hope and probably an unconscious realization that the end was near.

In the spring of 1930 the little people who thought of the "Crash" as a headline were reluctantly realizing that the creeping economic sickness would soon envelope them and they were searching for reassurance in worship and the familiar revival. The church was the only refuge in this "vast, evil city" that was faintly reminiscent of the life these people left in the small towns and on the farms of Georgia and Florida, so the two-week revival, now coming to its climax had been a rousing emotional, success if not a financial one.

Bethel AME Church was filled to capacity with its cooks, maids, wash-women, boarding house keepers, ditch diggers, stevedores, porters, bellhops, and a smattering of the "upper class"-- the secretaries and executives of the insurance company, the newspaper people and a few teachers. The women resplendent in their Sunday-go-to-meeting cocktail party finery and the men in unaccustomed suits, white shirts and ties fanned continuously to ease the heat of this very warm April Sunday that portended another hot, sticky Jacksonville summer.

As the strains of "Crying Holy" filtered softly and mournfully through the almost emotionally spent church of worshippers, the new members slowly filed forward and took their places across the front of the church facing the congregation to be welcomed through the Right Hand of Fellowship. Before the choir could begin to sing, this voice broke forth touching the souls of a passionate people. Bethel was not usually a shouting church so a sea of black, brown and tan faces turned indignantly and looked in wondering silence toward the gallery and my mother, Mattie Clayton.

Mama rose from her seat to the wide-eyed amazement of her sister Fanny and as if propelled by the unseen, she went down the steps to the vestibule, entered the church and walked toward the pulpit still singing. The affected reserve of the congregation, already penetrated, faded and the secret sorrows and apprehensions of each found expression in joining her in song.

It was a few months later when I was with Mama during her final illness that I heard the story. She was still a little bewildered by her behavior even after all of these weeks.

"I shouted, Hon," she said, "I don't know what on earth came over me," I was as astonished as Mama and Aunt Fanny

4

had been. Now, if it had been Aunt Fanny none of us would have given it a second thought. To Aunt Fanny the principle enjoyment of the church service was to get happy and shout.

Why did she do it? - My poor Mama. I thought it inconceivable that my Mama who was so mild mannered, who had borne everybody's troubles, who got even less, at least it seemed so, could have projected herself out of obscurity while in a church so far from her home in the red hills of Georgia.

Why, I have asked myself over and over again in these years since her death, did she live? Why did she who always somehow provided a refuge for others, never, after years of hope and planning and hard work have a refuge to call her own?

Even after death she is a constant solace and inspiration to me. I have dreamed of her often, though with diminishing frequency, through these years especially in my moments of despair, and they have been many. Often, I have awakened from a dream of her, sobbing as if my heart would break and saying, "My poor Mama, my poor Mama."

If I can find a reason for her all too short sojourn on this earth, it must be from those people whose lives she touched for she was surely one of those chosen to "Feed My Sheep."

Mama didn't remember her own mother, Maria Chandler Hamilton. She died when Mama was very small leaving eleven children. Her twin babies survived her only a few months. In those days of precarious child birth, a strong virile man often outlasted one or two wives. So it was with Grandpa Hamilton, It wasn't long after Grandma's death that he married Miss Laura and brought her home to tend his house and mother his brood. Miss Laura was a "big red woman" just as Grandma had been.

Grandpa was a farmer as were his sons after him. His rows of cotton stretched as far as the eye could see. This was his major crop. In the spring they made a blanket of pink blossoms which turned a tired green in the hot Georgia summer sun and then to snowy white as the pecan trees outlining the fields began to show promise of a fruitful autumn.

To Grandpa and his older children that snowy expanse meant long backbreaking hours of plowing, hoeing, fighting the insects and picking. The land had yet to be worn out and the harvests were plentiful.

A few years ago I went back to Sparta and found the old farm almost completely claimed by the red clay, eroded and producing scraggly weeds, a mute reproach to poor farming technique and years of neglect. The big rambling house was still standing beneath the chinaberry trees, unpainted and weather beaten. The long porch which separated the kitchen from the house was crumbling. Grandpa's third wife, then nearing ninety had been taken to the city by her grandchildren, who had long since realized the futility of trying to wrest an existence from the clay.

In 1888, this ghost ridden house which now groaned and complained when the wind whistled through her aching joints, was young, vibrant and alive, loving, and pleased to add Miss Laura's three children to her ample but now overflowing bosom.

Miss Laura wasn't by nature an affectionate woman and regarded her new charges as a necessary inconvenience. She was, however, efficient and soon had the house showing a woman's presence again. They all quickly made adjustments as there was always work to do -- clothes and dishes to wash, water to carry from the well, wood to cut, meals to prepare, cows to milk, chickens and stock to feed, eggs to gather, butter to churn, clothes to sew, night glasses to empty, lamp shades to clean, wicks to trim, fences to mend, meat to smoke, vegetables and fruit to pick and can and all of the endless work in the fields. So every able bodied child and adult was expected to do his share either in the field or at the house. When cotton picking time came, feeding the extra hands became a tremendous undertaking. Miss Laura solved it by having them eat in shifts without washing the plates. Being among the younger children, Mama was always in the second shift.

"Why ain't you eating Mattie?"

"Don't want it."

"Why don't you want it?" Very indignantly. "Ain't it good enough for you?"

"My plate ain't clean."

Very angrily, "You scornful devil, if you don't eat that you don't get anything."

This set the pattern of Mama's life for years to come. The quiet defiance of this little girl seemed a threat to Miss Laura's control of her household and she determined from that moment to break her spirit. So began Mama's years of loneliness.

Mama's older sister Willie, to whom she clung during these difficult days, fed her when Miss Laura wasn't looking and pleaded with her to try to pretend to do as Miss Laura said. But that quiet; honest strength that was to be her bulwark in the long night that was her life would not be assuaged. Willie was killed by lightening when Mama was seven.

One night Grandpa noticed how subdued and listless Mama had become and asked why.

"I'm hungry."

"Hungry?" he roared. "Much something t'eat there is round here and you hungry. What you talking bout chile? Laura!! What Mattie talking bout? She say she hungry."

"Mattie had her supper but she wouldn't eat it. All I can do is fix it," she said angrily.

"My plate was dirty," said Mama, tearfully.

Grandpa was a stern and loving father but remote because the problems of having three sets of children in the same house confused him so he solved them by avoiding them. He was too grateful to Miss Laura to risk offending her. After all it was a chore toting enough water for the needs of the house from the well and there were many people to feed, and what's a little dirt? Everybody has to eat a peck before he dies. But he did admonish Miss Laura to see that his children were well fed and repeatedly insisted that they all be sent to school.

At that, Miss Laura, sensing a victory but just to make sure, burst into tears and said she was doing the best she could. With so many children and one on the way she didn't see how she could do any better. The tears did their job well and Grandpa gathered his children around him and told them what a wonderful person Miss Laura was, and that they should do all they could to help her. The next day when Grandpa went to the field, Mama got a beating. From that day she kept her troubles to herself.

There was never a shortage of food on the farm but there was often a serious shortage of money for the necessities that couldn't be grown. However, Miss Laura was a very enterprising woman so during the slack farm seasons, she and the girls sewed piece work at home for a factory in town. Mama and Aunt Sally had to learn to sew when they were very young and fortunately so for Mama. When she was still a little girl in school, Miss Laura cut out her dresses and gave them to her to complete. Mama spent many agonizing hours trying often unsuccessfully to fit the pieces together in the right place. She eventually became quite competent after being humiliated in school by her meager, shoddy and ill fitting wardrobe to such an extent she stopped going in the fifth grade. Miss Laura insisted on the others going to school as Grandpa had requested, but she made no effort to encourage Mama to continue.

Aunt Sally and Uncle Buddy got along with Miss Laura just fine. They both knew how to snatch the most from life without regard for the consequences and they both knew how to temper their relationship with people with enough deceit and flattery to make the giver glad he gave, even though he knew he was being taken.

Uncle Buddy's methods with Miss Laura were even a bit more devious. He, very early, was a miniature replica of the man he was to become. He had a way with the ladies and a devil-may-care philosophy. He hid, not too well, his rascality behind his highly infectious smile. Miss Laura's affection for this virile youth was hardly maternal and he spent long hours in her room, routed occasionally when Grandpa returned unexpectedly early from his lodge meeting.

When Buddy decided to marry Julia, a refined and well bred

black (in the true sense) girl of good family, Miss Laura became very upset and raved as a woman betrayed by her lover. She said she would see Buddy George in hell before she would see him married to that "black devil." Buddy George married as he wished, but his life went on unaltered.

As she grew older and understood what was going on, Mama viewed this behavior with silent disgust, and the relationship between the wife and the oldest daughter at home became more strained. As the days, weeks and years passed, the unbearable became the usual and the senses became dulled and life went on.

Uncle Steve's free and reckless spirits wouldn't be bridled and he left home one spring day while in his middle teens to live with a woman in town. Steve was too straightforward to get along with Miss Laura and this was his way of escaping an intolerable situation. Even though he was very young, the family made only feeble attempts to break up this unhealthy alliance, as his going helped to ease the tension that developed as the boys grew older. Steve knew well his sister's plight and thought of her with growing concern as the summer wore into fall. He knew she could get the little soup tomatoes, carrots and other vegetables from the garden as long as the weather remained warm, but with the frost would come that agonizing constant hunger relieved only when Miss Laura was in a charitable mood. He timed his first trip home after hog killing when the smoke house was full. Miss Laura kept all of the farm keys on a chain at her waist, and refused to relinquish them to this farm boy playing Robin Hood very convincingly. He grabbed the axe and waved it menacingly and knocked the door down as she stood wringing her hands and screaming at him hysterically. After that he came periodically and took out enough to last Mama for days and cooked it for her; he wasn't afraid of Miss Laura. Mama always got a beating when he left but she always looked forward to his forays with grateful anticipation for it meant a full stomach for several days. She kept her food in a bag and took it with her to the fields, tossing it ahead of her as she chopped cotton. Often she had to brush the ants away before she could eat.

When the misery became acute between Steve's visits, Mama sometimes visited her Grandmother, who lived in a shack in the white folk's yard. There she got the love, attention and food she craved but that didn't last long for the old lady was even then, dying of cancer.

Occasionally her oldest brother, Bud and his wife let her stay with them for short periods. Bud was born before the end of slavery and was the master's son, but that was never discussed in our family. I learned little pieces of the truth through the years as a result of constant questioning. Uncle Bud was however, a true Hamilton in spirit and clung proudly to the name. These pleasant retreats always had to end and Mama had to go home.

One day when Mama was about fourteen Miss Laura came toward her with a strap to whip her for some obscure reason. In an instant her senses reeled in protest. In desperation she picked up a stick lying near, and dared her tormentor to touch her. Miss Laura stared at her stepchild in amazement for a moment, turned on her heel and strode into the house. Mama stood trembling, and suddenly afraid, then confident. She had won her freedom. From that day, Miss Laura ignored her, and life though lonely became a bit more tolerable.

Miss Laura and Grandpa had four children. She never fully recovered after the birth of the last one and was bedridden for many months. Miss Laura was ill over a period of time. Mama, being the oldest girl at home now, had the responsibility of caring for her and taking care of the younger children. These were Miss Laura's four and Mama's youngest brother and sister by her own mother. One day after Miss Laura had watched her go about her chores, she called her to the bed and bade her sit down.

"Mattie," she said "you are doing a very good job of seeing after me, keeping the house and looking after the children. Why do you take such good care of me? I often think of how I treated you children when I married your Papa. I was not very good to you, but since I've been down, I've prayed to God for forgiveness and I know my prayers have been answered. I'm not going to hell. I do worry about my little children. Mr. Hamilton is the kind of man who won't stay single long, and I worry all of the time when I think of anybody treating my little ones the way I treated you. Please Mattie, take care of my children. Please don't let them be abused," she cried, the sobs racking her wasted body.

The crumbling of the pride of this once arrogant woman was terrible to witness. Mama gave her promise, and went tearfully outside to cut the kindling to start dinner.

*   *   *

The foregoing was written in the summer of 1955. My mother, Georgia recalled the details of the story I had heard all of my life. She was recuperating from a mastectomy, and I was trying to rearrange the pieces of my life. The continuous conversation under the ash tree on West Street about Mama and all the kin folks was therapy for both of us.

Would that I had completed the story, for now I can only remember snatches of incidents, and in nothing that approaches chronological order.

It seems that the community was surprised when Mama and Papa married. Frank Clayton was a wild one. He liked fast women and fast horses. Nobody believed he could settle down with a quiet one like Mattie Hamilton. They had several children - seven I believe, including a set of twins. Mother was the third or fourth one. None of the others survived childhood. Most of them died at birth. Mother always marveled at her survival.

The Clayton home became the refuge of a stream of Mama's relatives. Uncle Steve killed a man and came to Mattie. She saw that he had the means with which to leave town. Aunt Sally married and produced two children, Mattieway and Julian. Sally's marriage was off again, on again so Mama reared the children. They were about Mother's age - Mattieway, a little older and Julian, a little younger. Uncle Buddy was the sporting uncle, the one that had the still. Buddy had several children. We met his daughter, Julia some years ago in Tallahassee.

There was the story about Papa getting religion. He saw a man on a white horse through the trees as he was praying in the woods. He came to town telling his religion - "He raised my feet out of the miry clay" etc. He didn't have religion long. Mama went to the A.M.E. Church in town while Papa went to the Baptist Church in the country. (Hancock County, Georgia)

Mother used to go to both churches. Mother was baptized as a baby in the AME church. The excitement was at Papa's church when his sisters got happy and shouted. One was known to walk the back of the pews when she was in her ecstasy. One preacher they had, named Natt was really great until he went to school. Then he couldn't preach anymore.

Mother was 14 and in the 9th grade in 1918 when the flu

pandemic occurred. There were deaths all over the county, and the public schools in Sparta closed. To keep from losing a year, she was sent to live with a cousin in Macon. There she attended Ballard, a private school, many of whose teachers were white missionaries from the North. In 1919 she returned to Sparta. Papa's cotton crop was good during World War I, so there was money to send Georgia to Morris Brown AME College in Atlanta for her last two years.

Papa was thirty-seven in 1917 and eligible for the draft but he said he wasn't mad with any Germans and he wouldn't "reddish." The family was scared to death that "they" would come to get him, but nobody did.

It was along about that time that Papa was driving his latest buggy (always the last word in buggies) down a narrow road in the county and he met a white man coming the other way. As was the custom in those days, he said, "Get out of my way Nigger," and raised his whip to hit Papa. Papa did what ever you do to horses to get them to go faster and ran the man off the road. The family sat tight, waiting for the lynch mob, but nothing happened.

Papa was a strong muscular man who could whip anybody in the county. Mother tells the story of him hitting a man in the front yard and the man reeled around the house until he fell in the back yard.

Papa never bought a house in Sparta. He said he wasn't going to buy a house for some other man's children (Mattieway and Julian) to live in. He rented his land in the country rather than sharecrop and had complete charge of the farm operation. The family lived in Sparta at the edge of the "Hill" – Hunt's Hill. Mama raised chickens and sold eggs. It was with her egg money that she was able to buy a small lot in Sparta.

Papa was a hard working man, if not a prudent one. He believed in the here-and-now rather than the what-might-happen. He made money during the war years and because the cotton crop was good in 1920, he rented more land, bought more machinery and sank all he had in the 1921 crop. The boll weevil got in the cotton. He lost all he had. The family left Sparta and went to Jacksonville, Florida to live. The story was, there were plenty of jobs in Jacksonville. Mother was then in school in Morris Brown, and they managed to keep her there to complete her schooling. She was taking a commercial course.

Papa would find work if there was any to be had, so was soon working. His brother, Eli soon followed to Jacksonville and Papa gave him his, Papa's, job. Papa was always sure he wouldn't be out of work long. He finally decided to buy a house in Jacksonville. For a few years they were free of worry. Then they found that the house they bought was heir's property. That revelation came in about 1929 when the world collapsed.

Mama died in 1930 - she was 46 years old. Papa was at loose ends. For a time he lived in Savannah near mother where he sold junk. Eventually he wandered back to Sparta and claimed the little lot that Mama had bought with her egg money. He built a little shack on the lot and died there alone in 1938. He was 58 years old.

Papa's father was named Mack. He could never decide whether his last name was Baxter, White, or Clayton. Papa called himself Clayton. We decided that he must have been troublesome if he was sold so many times, but that picture doesn't quite fit with his going with his master to fight on the Confederate side of the Civil war.

Papa's mother was named Maria. She had several children. The only names I know are Lou and Eli. I have written Annie B. Barnes who was Papa's niece, but I didn't get much information, and I didn't write again.

My Mother and Me

My Mother and Me

Some of the older folks in Sparta Georgia along about the nineteen teens called her the "smartest child in Hancock County." This round faced, brown skinned girl with kinky hair and a flattish nose was my mother, Georgia Frank Clayton. She was born on February 15, 1904 and was one of several children born to Frank (1878-1936) and Mattie Hamilton Clayton (1884-1930).

She was the Clayton's only child to survive past infancy, and her parents adored her. Adoration in those days didn't lead to relief from chores - and there were plenty of chores in the small house that they lived in on a dirt road on the edge of Sparta. There was no plumbing. Water was fetched from a well in the yard, and the outhouse was out beyond the garden.

Papa Clayton was a farmer. He didn't own his land but rented it. He was not a sharecropper. He worked hard and his fortunes rose and fell according to the success of his cotton crop. Mama Clayton kept a small vegetable garden and chickens at the home, which was also rented. If Papa had lived in this day, he would have driven a Cadillac. Mother[1] always said that her Papa[2] liked beautiful buggies and fast horses.

He successfully resisted buying land because he didn't want

---

[1] "Mother" refers to Georgia Clayton Gordon, our mother.
[2] "Papa" refers to Frank Clayton, our grandfather.

to buy for other people's children. Mama[3] had a procession of relatives to come to stay for a while. Papa resented them, especially Mattieway and Julian who were the children of Mama's sister, Sally Robinson. Those children lived with the Claytons for long periods of time. However, Mama never lost her desire for a home of her own. She sold vegetables and eggs for many years and eventually saved enough to buy a small building lot in Sparta.

In the summer when Papa hired extra help there was always a noon meal to cook for the hands. This meant chopping kindling to build a fire in the wood cook stove. Preparing fried chicken meant killing the chickens, dipping them in boiling water, then in cold water to loosen the feathers, picking the feathers off, removing the entrails, taking care to carefully cut the bile off of the livers, cutting into serving sized pieces, seasoning, flouring, then cooking in hot grease.

Preparing vegetables meant picking, cleaning, sometimes shelling, securing meat from the smoke house for seasoning, then cooking in water until very soft. These meals always included corn bread and/or biscuits, and desserts. Upland Georgia can be brutally hot in the summer. Even with all of the large shade trees and all the windows and doors open, cooking a midday meal on a wood stove in the summer in Georgia could be

---

[3] "Mama" refers to Mattie Clayton, our grandmother.

miserable. As a preteen, Mother was expected to help with the cooking and help with the washing of the dishes afterward.

Mother didn't often tend the cotton. In one of her stories, she reported picking one hundred pounds of cotton in one day including sticks stones and other debris. Her girl cousins could pick one hundred pounds by noon and another one hundred pounds in the afternoon. There were lots of cousins because Mama had twenty-one sisters and brothers and Papa had eight sisters and brothers, and they all had children.

Chores slowed in winter. During the school term Mother's lessons came before the chores. Some of Mama's relatives predicted that little Georgia Frank would never amount to a hill of beans with so much coddling. Mama never went past the fifth grade in school but she had a healthy respect for education, and she was determined that her child would go as far in school that she wanted to.

Mother soaked up all she observed like a sponge. She excelled in all she tried but one dream she had in elementary school never came to be. In those days (even until my own elementary school days) schools presented an annual operetta, typically a fairy tale such as *Cinderella* or *Sleeping Beauty*. The princess was always played by one of the little girls who lived on the "Hill." These little girls had long curly hair and were fair of face. According to Mother, none of them could sing and dance as well as she, but she was never chosen. Strangely, the boy friends she chose as a young teenager were always of the same families that produced the princesses. One of them lived in Dublin as an adult and I met him there after Daddy died. He looked very much like Daddy.

Mother may have been passed over in school, but she shone in the local churches where she was called on to perform in various programs. Mama was A.M.E. and Mother was baptized as a baby as Methodist. Papa's church in the country was Baptist. Mother often attended both churches on a Sunday. The action was at Papa's church where his sisters got happy and shouted. Aunt Fannie was known to walk the back of the pews when in her ecstasy. It was in Papa's church that Mother honed her mimicking skills. She could preach with the best of them, and could sing with soul.

In 1918 there was an influenza pandemic. People were dying from the flu all over the world. The public schools in Sparta closed. Mother was sent to Macon to live with a cousin, whose name I don't remember, to finish out the term. Macon, though a little town, was a whole lot bigger than Sparta, which was a dot on the map. There Mother attended Ballard, a private school many of whose teachers were white missionaries from the north. There were many schools like Ballard allover the south. They were established soon after the Civil War to educate and socialize the newly emancipated slaves.

Macon and Ballard became Mother's first exposure to a more genteel life away from a Georgia cotton farm. At school there were more books to read and Mother soaked it all up. She found a particular liking for English novels. At her cousin's home there was electricity for lighting, and her water well was conveniently located on her back porch.

In 1919 Mother returned to Sparta for one more year of schooling. Papa's cotton crops were abundant during World War I and brought high prices. Papa prospered so there was money to send Mother to Morris Brown College in Atlanta for her last two years of high school. It was common in those days for Black colleges in the south to offer schooling from grades one through college. These colleges attracted boarding students from small and not so small towns where the public educational experience for colored people was minimal.

At age sixteen Mother wanted to be a secretary so she took the commercial course. Georgia Clayton loved Morris Brown where there was running water, electric lights, central heating, meals that she didn't have to cook, and people like her. There she met our father, Bob Gordon. Daddy[4] had many girlfriends -- the long curly-haired kind. Mother's boyfriend was Jack Dasher, Daddy's room-mate. Sometimes, Mother helped one of Daddy's

---

[4] "Daddy" refers to Robert "Bob" Gordon, our father.

wannabe girlfriends to write letters to him.

The summer before Mother's senior year in 1921 the boll weevil got in the cotton. Because Papa's crops had been phenomenal during the previous two years he over-extended himself. He bought a lot of new machinery to be paid for at crop's end. There was no crop and he was financially ruined. He and Mama moved to Jacksonville, Florida because jobs were said to be plentiful there.

Somehow Mother's parents managed to keep her in school until she graduated a commercial high school course at Morris Brown in 1922. Mother returned home, not to Sparta, but to Jacksonville, called by Mama, "a big evil city." Mother's job search that summer led her to a school in Thunderbolt, Georgia. Thunderbolt is now a bedroom community of Savannah. Then, it was a small fishing village surrounded by woods. The school, called Central Park College, was supported by the A.M.E. Church. It was composed of grades one through twelve. Mother taught fifth and sixth grades. The students and teachers lived in a dormitory on the campus. The students came from rural areas in the state of Georgia where there were no public schools for colored people.

Mother approached her job with fervor, which is characteristic of the way she lived her life. She would try anything. In addition to teaching her classes she produced a play, *East Lynne*, influenced by those English novels, and organized and directed a choir. Somewhere along the way Mother must have had piano lessons of some kind. I can't believe she taught herself. Maybe she did, for while her right hand was fairly accurate on the piano, the left hand did its own thing.

Then in fall of 1923, who would come to teach mathematics at Central Park but Bob Gordon. He came with his new college degree from Morris Brown. As usual, according to Mother, the girls there swooned over the new professor, but he courted Mother. They planned to marry in Cleveland, Ohio in the summer of 1924. Mother had planned to visit cousins in Cleveland and Detroit. Daddy planned to visit his sister, Mayo (May Olivia) in Cleveland, and his sister, Lillie in Detroit. During America's experience with World War I (1917-1918) hordes of southern blacks moved northward to work in war industries. Most of them remained in northern cities after the war. So it was with our parent's relatives. Mother enjoyed her time in Detroit.

In 1924 the Harlem Renaissance was in full flower. Blacks were being recognized for their contributions in music, in literature, and in the theater. Paul Robeson was appearing on Broadway in "The Emperor Jones." These were exhilarating times for black people and the mood spread to other cities in the north. Over time, the scope of the movement widened to include most of the country. This was the time of the Charleston, the

Black Bottom, and the Boll Weevil Cut Out. Prohibition gave rise to "bath tub gin." Women smoked, and wore their dresses above their knees. According to Mother, all of this frenzy was a bit much for a girl from Sparta, Georgia, population 3,000. She was not up to the rigors of Black recreation in Detroit. She said she went to sleep while others danced. I don't know if I believed her. I know she loved to dance, and she had an insatiable curiosity about almost everything.

I gather that Cleveland wasn't as raucous as Detroit. Cleveland was where Mother was supposed to marry Daddy, but he didn't show up. I didn't hear this part of the story until just before Mother died. She never told me his excuse for not showing up and I didn't ask him. How they survived the standup and resumed their engagement, I'll never know. Anyway, they were married in Jacksonville at her parent's home on Christmas Day, 1924. Mother didn't tell me anything about the wedding - what they wore, who was there, or what they ate.

After the holiday, they returned to Central Park and resumed teaching. However, they were not being paid. The school was having serious financial problems. Mother was never one to wait to see what might happen. She went to Savannah and got a job as a secretary to the president of the black bank. I think it was called the Wage Earner's Bank. The president, named Scott also owned three movie theaters. They were the Dunbar, the Star, and one other. After Mother obtained a job in Savannah, Daddy approached Scott for a job and became the manager of the three silent movie theaters. Daddy and Mother rented a cottage at 712 W. 53rd Street (Victory Drive) in Savannah from Mr. and Mrs. Golden who lived two doors away in a brick two-story house.

The halcyon period of their lives began in 1925 and lasted five years. They were able to make friends of their age group in Savannah and they learned to play bridge. Daddy refused to go to dances and didn't like Mother dancing. She learned bridge so that they would have a shared recreation.

They went to Forsythe to visit his family in that small Georgia town east of Macon. Looking back over a long ago coy conversation, I think Mother was trying to tell me that I was conceived in Forsythe in a cotton field among the blossoms. This visit introduced Mother to the family of her new husband. Papa Gordon, who was born around 1850, and was half white. He died in the early 1920s. Mama Gordon was born around 1855. (These dates are according to Michael) Her ancestry was black, white and Native American. She was probably half black. George and Mary Morse Gordon had nine children, two boys and seven girls. Our father, Robert Lee was the youngest. The children ranged in color from brown to white. Or from Lillie and Bub (George, Jr.) to Morsey. Their hair ranged in texture from crinkly to straight. Or, from Hookie (Burma) to Morsey. The others were Sarah, May Olivia, Ruth, and Olive.

In the fullness of time Mother went to Jacksonville to Mama's house to await the birth of her first child. I was born at the home on Kings Road on February 23, 1926. I was told that my arrival occurred on Monday at 1 P.M. The day of the week does not correspond with actuality. I weighed ten pounds, and the gene distribution was unfortunate. I had the body build, color, and hair like my mother; and singing and athletic skills like my father. However with my grandmother prodding my mother to talk to me, I modified my morose look and was ready to go to Savannah when I was six weeks old.

Mother spent the next four years teaching me things that I could learn. Actually I turned out to be a rather attractive little girl who couldn't carry a tune and could skip on only one foot. When Mother was invited to sing on various programs at churches, I was also invited to do my thing. So I was taught poems at a very early age. The first was:

> Good Morning Merry Sunshine
> What makes you wake so soon?
> You scare the little stars away
> And shine away the moon
> I saw you go to sleep last night
> When I ceased my praying
> How did you get way up there
> And where have you been staying?

My Mother and Me

I soon had several more sophisticated poems in my reper-
toire. None of that helped me when I went with Mother to her
bridge club meetings. Some of the ladies had little girls that they
brought with them. We were expected to play together. Typically, three year old children don't play together long before
they fight, and I was beat up. When I complained to Mother
about being hit, she would say, "Hit them back." The next time
we went, I got hit and I went running to Mother saying, "Evadne
hit me back." Of course, Evadne's mother thought I was an un-
reasonable child who thought she could hit and not get hit back.
Mother could not make her understand what I meant. I guess
that was the first indication that I wasn't ever going to have
"street smarts."

Sometimes Mother and I went to the theater in the late afternoon to see the movie and wait for Daddy to finish his duties for
the night. My most vivid memory of the theater was that people
ate fish sandwiches as they watched the movie. Savannah was,
and still is, a beautiful seacoast town with charm. Men pushed
carts through the streets loaded with good things to eat from the
sea. Women sold crabs on the street from baskets carried on
their heads. On Saturday night on some street corners a heating
unit made of a large oil drum was set up, a charcoal fire was
made, a grill was inserted, fish were fried, and fish sandwiches
were sold. In our section of the city the numbered streets had

plats down the center. On some streets live oaks graced the plats, but on our street, Victory Drive, palm trees caught the breeze there.

During this period, my parents like most of the rest of the country were prospering. Papa, in Jacksonville was making money. He probably worked as a stevedore on the docks since he was strong, willing to work, and had very little education. He finally decided to buy the house on Kings Road, and he gave Mother a player piano. She was delighted for she loved music and she played the piano and sang as a way of life.

Georgia State College for Negroes, now called Savannah State was in Thunderbolt and could be reached by street car. Mother decided to take some college courses. Of course, I went with her to school. I told everybody that I was going to college and was taking French and English. By that time we had acquired a cat whose name was French. The cat and I were not friends. She would spit at me and jump on top of the piano where I couldn't reach her.

Mother became pregnant twice during this period. The first ended in a miscarriage. The second was stillborn. I am told that the stillborn child looked like Aunt Sarah, which meant she looked white.

I have a few memories of my life before 1930. Memories like eating Fig Newtons because they were the only cookies that

I was allowed to eat; getting fish bones removed from my throat by the doctor across the street; Mama coming to visit from Jacksonville; us visiting Jacksonville where I rode in a buggy.

I have put off writing about the years 1930 - 1932 because I always feel sad when I think about it. It was a period of agony for the young Gordon couple. Perhaps I should celebrate the period for they survived it and went on to rear a great family.

The whole country was in despair beginning with the stock market crash in 1929 that ushered in the Great Depression. In Jacksonville, jobs on the docks dried up. Papa was often out of work. The house on Kings Road turned out to be heirs' property, and our grandparents lost their investment. This was before there were laws protecting the consumer. Then Mama died of dropsy in the spring of 1930 at the age of 46. Mother was devastated. She mourned for her mother all the days of her life.

Soon after Mama died, life for the Gordons in Savannah began to unravel. About that time Daddy took his family to Forsythe to visit. While there he painted his mother's house. On the return to Savannah he announced that he was no longer working at the theaters. He never said why. The school, Central Park had closed. Jobs were almost nonexistent. He tried writing insurance. His territory was in Thunderbolt, to which he walked from Savannah.

Mother took a class in Poro, a hair dressing system that rivaled Madame Walker. I still have two of the straightening combs that she acquired. She tried doing hair but it didn't work out. Neither Daddy nor Mother could make any money and the bills piled up. (As a young child I had no idea of the tension that must have existed in those days.) Then Mother learned that the Breakers Hotel in Palm Beach, Florida was hiring maids for the high season. She was hired for January through March of 1931. She went to Florida to work even though she was already pregnant with Bobby.

At that time, Aunt Sarah lived in Savannah where she cooked for a white family. Aunt Sarah was an exceptional cook. At one time, she and her husband, Mr. DeFord owned a restaurant in Savannah. She made the best lady-fingers. Mother's friend, Ethel Jenkins, who by the way was a relative of B.B. Barnwell, lived near our house. Aunt Sarah and Ethel took care of me while Daddy walked to Thunderbolt.

Mother was sick most of the time that she was in Palm Beach but she persevered to the end. The experience opened new vistas for her, a window on how the rich really lived. She saw what they ate, how they dressed, how they behaved. She, however, didn't last long with actual contact with the guests because she wasn't subservient enough in her demeanor. For example, when she didn't hear or didn't understand an order she would reply, "I beg your pardon" instead of the expected reply,

"Ma'am?" So she spent most of her time behind the scenes making beds or preparing vegetables. The people who could say, "Ma'am?" made the most money.

Mother returned to Savannah at the end of March very much pregnant and sick. Since she had already lost two babies she was determined to keep this one. Conventional wisdom said, once begun, miscarriages would continue to occur unless certain precautions were taken. On doctor's orders, she remained in bed much of the time to make sure that this child would be born at the depth of the depression into a home where there was no money. Papa Clayton remarked that the baby's name ought to be, "Depress."

Papa had moved to Savannah and had rented a room nearby. He pushed a cart and sold junk. Ever a man of the soil, he made a deal with a man who owned a vacant lot and planted a garden there. That garden kept us in vegetables all the summer and fall.

Days after Bobby was born, I came down with a terrible stomach ache which the doctor across the street diagnosed as appendicitis. He prescribed ice packs to the affected area. Mother, even with a new baby, spent days and nights putting ice packs on me. I didn't get any better so the doctor recommended hot applications. That didn't work so we went back to the ice packs.

Days passed and I was a sick five-year-old. Finally, Mother

asked around for a recommendation for a doctor. She was led to a Dr. Skinner, a surgeon who immediately put me in the hospital and operated. I am told that during the surgery, a cup of pus was removed from my body cavity. I was in the hospital for six weeks before I returned to my family. I immediately blamed Aunt Sarah for giving me appendicitis. She had plaited my hair too tight.

I don't remember going to church during the first five and a half years of my life. I don't remember my parents going to church. I never knew how Daddy happened to meet Father Brown who was the priest at St Augustine's on the West Side of Savannah. At that time there were two Black Episcopal churches there. The other one on the East Side was St. Stephen's. But meet Father Brown he did, and Daddy's life and ours were radically changed. Because of Father Brown's influence, Daddy decided to go to Bishop Payne Seminary in Petersburg, VA to become an Episcopal priest.

He left in September of 1931. Mother, Bobby and I remained in Savannah in the cottage at 712 West Victory Drive. I didn't see the furniture leave. Suddenly we were living with Mr. and Mrs. Golden in the brick house up the street. It was many years later that I learned that the furniture was repossessed. It had been pawned, including Mother's piano. We did get to keep the bedroom furniture, including the rocking chair, the long table that had been placed beneath the living room window, pots, pans, eating utensils, china, and personal mementos.

By this time the bill for my hospital expenses came due and the surgeon's bill came also. I can't tell you how the hospital bill got paid or if it was, but Mother took a job as Dr. Skinner's maid and baby sitter in order to pay him. She also worked at night at a tea room in downtown Savannah. She was hired as a waitress but her demeanor again forced her into the kitchen. I guess Mrs. Golden sat with us during the day. I remember Papa sitting with me at night and making corn cakes and telling ghost stories.

In later years Mother told me of how she walked home at night from downtown Savannah crying and praying. She was always composed when I saw her. At the time, I was not aware of her agony. In fact she often joked about how the Skinner children would escape the house and run down the street half clothed. Mother would have to chase them and she would hope that no one she knew would see her in her maid's uniform chasing those little white children. In case you didn't know it, your mother was a proud woman. At that time she was twenty-seven years old.

I have very little memory of the winter of 1931-32. I can't remember Christmas at all. I do have two distinct memories of the spring. One event was the newspaper extras on the street when the Lindbergh baby was kidnapped. Yes, the newsboys yelled, "Extra, extra, read all about it!" The other event was watching it rain on a nearby corner while the sun was shining everywhere else.

Finally the school year was over and Daddy was back in Savannah. However, his required internship was at a small church in Albany, Georgia that had no rector. We all went to Albany on the train. In those days Black people in the south rode in train cars that were directly behind the baggage cars. There was no air conditioning and windows were raised to catch the breeze. The breeze brought relief from the heat and also brought coal dust from the coal-burning engine. Colored people, as we were called in those days, sat in the back of the bus but were privileged to sit at the front of the train.

The backs of the seats on the train were movable, and probably still are, so that the car can go in the opposite direction without turning the car around. So it was easy for us to be seated on two seats that faced each other. We carried our lunch in a shoe box so that we didn't have to purchase lunch on the train or in depots along the way.

I was over six years old at the time. That meant I was slightly above the age to ride free. My parents agreed that I was to ride as under six. After we settled in our seats I was told to lie down on the seat. I did that and Mother placed a small blanket over my legs. When the conductor came to take our tickets, I rose up and grinned at him showing no upper front teeth. It was out of character for me to grin at strangers. My parents were mortified and afraid they would have to buy a half price ticket for me, but we escaped.

In 1932 Albany was a small sleepy town with dirt streets in the neighborhood where we lived. Pecan trees were profuse. We lived with Mrs. Bentley, an older lady who normally lived alone in a big rambling house. The only detail I remember about the house was a large screened-in back porch where we did lots of family things. Mother's girlhood friend, Louvenia Dyer lived in Albany. Louvenia had two daughters about my age. She and Mother often washed our hair on that porch. We played games there. I spent the summer getting ready for school in the fall. I had reading and arithmetic lessons. Mother gave me peanuts for spelling words correctly. Bobby turned one year old on July 21, 1932. He was a pleasant little baby who enjoyed going to church. Whenever he was put in his stroller and pushed along he would yell, "Church, church." He talked well for a child his age but he couldn't or wouldn't walk. Mother got a little concerned since I had walked at ten months and nobody ever called me agile. A neighbor suggested rubbing doodle bugs on Bobby's knees. I was sent under the house to look for the small conical depressions in which doodle bugs lived. I took a small stick and jiggled it in the depression saying, "Doodle bug, doodle bug your house is on fire," and the doodle bug appeared. I soon had several of the ugly little things to rub on Bobby's knees. It didn't work. Bobby walked when he was good and ready at thirteen months.

When the summer was over we headed for Petersburg. I don't remember if we went back through Savannah or if we traveled on the train from Albany to Petersburg. We were to live in student housing there. Married students lived in a duplex, more accurately called a double tenement. The duplex was on Wilcox Street around the comer from the divinity school that was located on West Street.

The Bishop Payne Divinity School on West Street was established by the Episcopal Church to train Black clergy to lead Black Episcopal congregations. The work toward the Bachelor of Divinity (B.D) degree took three years. Matriculation for this degree followed a B.S. or B.A. degree from a college. Now, there is no graduate B.D. degree. Now, the degree awarded is appropriately called the Master of Divinity.

The school had four buildings. They were the chapel (the only building still standing) at the corner of West and Wilcox; the Warden's residence at 411 S. West Street; a dormitory next door where the candidates without their wives with them lived; and across the street was the classroom and library building. The enrollment was typically very small. Each class had four or five members that led to a total enrollment of twelve to fifteen. I knew most of the men by their last names and called them that.

We lived in a gray painted dwelling. It was a two story house with two bedrooms and bath upstairs and two rooms downstairs. The larger room downstairs was what is now called a great room. It had a coal stove for heating. The smaller room was a kitchen with a coal-burning cook stove. There were grates in the ceiling above the stoves to carry the heat upstairs. I can't remember the furniture. But I do remember the radio. We always had a radio. Amos and Andy came on at 7 p.m. and Lum and Abner at 7:15. At 7:30 I had to get ready to go to bed and be in bed by 8 o'clock. Children had bed times in those days.

As I was six and a half, it was appropriate for me to begin school in fall of 1932. I did not begin in the fall of 1931 because at five and a half I was too young to begin school in Savannah. Savannah did not have half-year promotions but Petersburg did at that time. I was enrolled at Giles B. Cook Primary School and tested to determine my beginning level. I could read, spell, and do arithmetic so I was put in 2-H, the second half of second grade. Everything went well at the beginning of the day. New girls do not have it as bad as new boys at a new school. Mrs. Johnson, the principal of the little school was my teacher. The lessons were easy for me except for one problem. At the end of the day Mrs. Johnson would put the next day's assignment on the board for us to copy. I could print but I could not write cursively. The others had already started to learn cursive writing. Mother had not taught me how to write. Consequently in those first days, I could never complete copying my assignment down and I would go home crying. I finally learned to scribble enough to know what was required. I never did learn how to do that elegant Palmer handwriting.

Each school day began with devotions. Typically, we said a prayer in unison. This was followed by individual Bible verses. I didn't know any Bible verses but that deficiency was quickly taken care of. The devotions ended with the singing of a hymn. After devotions came cleanliness inspection. We were required to bring a handkerchief to school each day. Since I didn't have a handkerchief, Mother made one for me out of a piece of organdy. Have you ever tried to use an organdy handkerchief? (I don't remember seeing any tissues in that day). We placed our hands on the handkerchief while the teacher inspected row by row. Our nails were required to be clean and shaped.

I have spotty memories of the two years we spent in Petersburg, Apparently the Diocese of Georgia financed Daddy's stay at the seminary. In those days many of the parishes in the national church subsidized seminarians and priests assigned to mission churches. Each year the seminarian or priest would make a request to a donor parish for clothes for himself, his wife and each minor child. The arrival of these clothes in a box delivered by railway express was a much anticipated event. The "box" usually came in the fall of the year. Daddy did maintenance work at the seminary for spending money. We didn't have much money but our basic needs were met. There seemed to have been no financial worries.

The black residents of Petersburg were friendly toward the seminarians and their families. Some of the local women found husbands at Bishop Payne. The social climate was great for our parents and they found friends in Petersburg. Mrs. Lizzie Griffin became Mother's lifelong friend.

Just before our first Christmas in Petersburg when I was almost seven, I declared that there was no Santa Claus. My reasoning was that there were too many Santas on every corner during the season. And furthermore they didn't sound like the one on the radio. I may have been seeking reassurance but I didn't get it from my parents. They were so proud of my reasoning ability. Or was it because I wouldn't thereafter need many presents? That was the Christmas that I requested and received a pair of roller skates. Christmas morning I proudly joined all the children with skates on the sidewalk in front of Payne on West Street. I promptly fell, hurt my arm and never put skates on again.

Fast-forward about forty years when our granddaughter, Kim

was six almost seven. She and our nephew, Charles spent the summer with us on Sheffield Place in Ettrick. Kim had a new pair of skates and was learning to skate in our driveway. Her Granddaddy held her steady while she tried skating toward me. As she seemed to have good balance, he let her go. She continued toward me and lost her balance. My feet were parted as I reached to catch her. She rolled between my legs and fell backward. I grabbed her to break her fall and I fell over her cracking my head on the pavement. It raised a bump on my head the size of an egg. Since then, not only have I not tried to skate, I have stayed away from anybody on skates. Kim was not hurt at all.

It was in Petersburg that Mother decided to straighten my hair. Before that I was treated to a whole lot of Vaseline, water, and brushing to make my hair that was supposed to be curly, stay down. The change came because there were girls in Petersburg who had "better" hair than mine who had their hair straightened.

Before the first year in Petersburg was over, Mother was pregnant again. We could not accompany Daddy to Albany again for his summer internship. Instead Mother, Bobby and I moved into the vacant student dormitory of Bishop Payne Divinity School. The students had gone for the summer. The dormitory facilities were spacious and convenient while we waited for the new baby. The new baby, Ronald Clayton

Gordon, was born on August 13, 1933. Mother couldn't quite bring herself to call him Ronald Coleman Gordon after the popular movie star of the time.

There was a young lady who came in to help us during that summer of 1933. Her name was Gwendolyn. I can remember only one event concerning Gwendolyn. Mother sent her to the store to get grocery items that included crackers. I went with her. She bought crackers. Mother was expecting cookies. We didn't use the term cookies in Georgia. I was supposed to tell Gwendolyn what Mother meant.

Ronald was a big, robust baby who required being rocked to sleep by Daddy. He would eat anything including the paint off his crib. It is a wonder he didn't get lead poisoning. When Ronald was six months old, Mother became pregnant with George and Ronald was weaned from her breast. Mother breast-fed all of her babies. She was sick most of her pregnancy with George so Daddy became Ronald's primary care taker.

Petersburg had snowy winters in the thirties. On our second and last Christmas in Petersburg I wanted a sled. Of course it was not practical for me to have a sled because when school was over we would begin our journey to Tallahassee, Florida with a stopover in Savannah. Daddy was to begin his ministry at St. Michael and all Angels Church in Tallahassee. He was indebted to the Diocese of Georgia for his education but there were no openings there.

I can remember three whippings that I got as a child. The first was in Petersburg. My job was to put Bobby's shoes on his feet. He would curl his toes so I couldn't get his shoes on so I bit him. The second time was in the Savannah stopover on our way to Tallahassee. We were again at Mrs. Golden's house. There was a large chinaberry tree in the back yard and also various varieties of grass. I was playing in the back and found an old spoon. I crushed some of the chinaberries, stirred in some grass, and added a little dirt and water. This was the "medicine" that I gave Bobby. This medicine was probably why Bobby was free of the childhood diseases that the other boys had. He had a built-in immunity. The third whipping was in Tallahassee.

The train trip to Tallahassee must have been a hoot with three children and one on the way. I was most impressed with changing trains in Jacksonville. I had not remembered the display in the station of alligators, oranges and other Florida products in my previous trips to Jacksonville when I was much younger.

In 1934, Tallahassee, the capital of Florida had a population of about 15,000. Many of the streets in the black community were unpaved. St. Michael and All Angels Church was on a corner facing a paved street, South Boulevard. The street to the left of the church was also paved. I believe it was named Lafayette.

Two blocks up Lafayette was the Capitol. There was a mansion on the street parallel to Boulevard behind us. The grounds of the mansion were extensive. The foliage was dense with pecan trees and banana trees. A chain link fence separated our grounds from the grounds of the mansion. The first block of the street leading to the Capitol was lined, on our side, with pecan trees. There was also a deep drainage ditch instead of curbs. There was no sidewalk. Walking toward the capitol on the block next to the mansion was to an eight-year-old like walking through the woods. There was a sidewalk on the other side of the street where white people lived. The center of the whole block of South Boulevard in front of our house was occupied by a curb market. Farmers came there on Wednesday and Saturday to sell produce. The ubiquitous pecan trees lined the market in front of our dwelling. Tallahassee then and even in 1975 when Goody and I visited there gave the impression of lush greenery. There were trees everywhere.

The church was a white frame building that needed painting. We were to live in the annex that was built, I suppose, to be the parish hall. We walked with our luggage into a large room beyond which was a smaller long room with a toilet down one end. There was a commode and sink, but no bathtub. The kitchen had a small coal-burning cooking stove but no water. There was a water faucet outside the kitchen window. We children, Bobby,

47

Ronald and I raced around looking at things. Mother sat down on one of the big trunks that followed us around and cried. That was the first among the very few times that I saw her cry. This move probably occurred in August of 1934. George was born in that house on November 4.

But life went on. Daddy went out to a second-hand store and bought an ice-box and some cots and mattresses. I don't remember how he managed that. We had no transportation or telephone. He may have had previous communication with one or more of the few members of the church. Those beds were the source of our eight-year acquaintance with bed bugs.

It wasn't long after we settled in that a note written in red ink was pushed under our front door inviting us to leave. It was signed, KKK. You have to be black and living in the Deep South to know the terror generated by a Ku Klux Klan threat. We were living on the wrong side of the street. The street we lived on separated the black community from the white community in that part of town. The colored people lived on the other side of the curb market. Daddy took the note to a local judge that had a policeman stationed on our corner for a while. I felt safe. Little did I know that at that time, a policeman would not necessarily protect us from the Klan.

I started to school after Labor Day. Somehow there was enough money to pay the small tuition for me to go to the Model

School on the edge of the campus of the then Florida A. and M. College (FAMC). I was eight-and-a-half. I don't remember the first day. I suppose Daddy must have taken me and we must have walked. FAMC was a "fur" piece from us, straight down Boulevard, down the steps to cross the railroad tracks, up a red clay hill to finally reach the top where FAMC stood on the edge of town. My school was the practice school for training elementary school teachers. The public school for colored could be reached by going the other way, up Boulevard. The distance was about the same. I had been promoted to 4H in Petersburg. There were no half-year classes in Tallahassee so I was tested to determine if I would be placed in 4th grade or 5th grade. I was placed in 5th grade.

My memories of the first year are spotty. I could check books out of the college library. I started reading the Jhalna novels during that time. The college cafeteria for day students sold veal cutlet sandwiches for 15 cents. Hot dogs were 5 cents, and hamburgers were a dime. I carried my sandwiches from home. All students from fourth grade through college marched to the auditorium following behind the college band every Wednesday at noon. After devotions, the president, J.R.E. Lee would, very often, speak. Other times there would be an educational program. All female students would wear blue skirts and white blouses. The male students wore dark suits and white shirts. If they were in R.O.T.C. they wore the uniform.

Getting through that first winter in Tallahassee with a new baby and an impossible house must have strained the patience and ingenuity of our parents. Soon after school opened the fall rains began. It seemed we were always getting the tail of hurricanes. The roof of the church annex that was our abode was like a sieve and water poured in. When it rained we had to use most of our pots to catch the downpour.

Tallahassee had another peculiarity of Florida, cock roaches, huge flying ones. This was before the age of strong pesticides, so fighting vermin was a major problem. Just living took up a lot of time and energy. St. Michael's had been dormant for years. Therefore, soon after our arrival Daddy began to introduce himself to the former members. The names I remember are Dr. and Mrs. Campbell and their daughters, Alpha, Zillah and Laura Belle; Mr. And Mrs. Adderley and sons Nathaniel and Julian (who both became jazz musicians); the Spearmans and children Rawn, Viva, Olivia, Ohara, Leonard and two others; Mrs. Baker and daughters Jacqueline and Barbara (her husband, Dr. Baker and son, Billy were Baptists); Vinzant Pottsdammer; Mrs. Lomas, the grand dame who had a car with a rumble seat. The Joneses and their five children (Constance, three boys and a small girl) began attend church and were confirmed in due time.

The small white frame church was built in the typical Anglican tradition. The organ was operated by foot pedals and needed tuning. For a while the church organist was Mrs. Shirley whose husband was the priest at a church in Apalachicola. She was in Tallahassee pursuing a degree at FAMC. The Shirleys were the parents of Don Shirley, a jazz pianist of a few decades ago.

Before I go on about the development of St. Michael's as seen through my eyes I must tell you about washing clothes. I can't remember how we washed in Savannah or in Petersburg. Washing machines were not in general use. But, I remember Tallahassee. On washday (Monday) Daddy made a fire in the back yard and placed a tub on bricks over the fire. He filled the tub with a garden hose attached to that one faucet. In the meantime Mother separated the clothes (all cotton) into piles, white in one pile and colored in another. Dirty diapers were pre-washed in a slop jar.

There were three wash tubs on benches beside the back of the house. In the first tub we washed the white clothes on a washing board with Octagon soap until clean. The clothes were then placed in the tub of boiling water over the fire for sterilization and further cleaning. They were then removed from the hot water with a heavy stick (an old broom handle) and placed in the first rinse tub, and swished around. Then they were wrung out, put in the last rinse water with bluing, swished around, wrung out all by hand and hung on the line. All of the white clothes had to be sparkling white. We used a lot of Clorox, but not too much. The babies would get diaper rash if the Clorox was not rinsed properly. There always seemed to be a baby. After the white clothes came the colored clothes. The water in the rinse tubs was changed at least once to keep the clothes fresh smelling. When the colored were hung on the line they had to be color coordinated. No matter how third world our circumstances were, we expected to maintain a cultured appearance. I have no memory of how all of this was accomplished during that first winter. I was a part of the proceedings during that first summer (1935).

By the fall of 1935 things eased up. Daddy got a job as principal of a two-teacher school that met in a church in Leon County. We got an inside sink in the kitchen; we purchased a new oil burning modern cook stove; and Daddy bought a car. The car was a 1929 Chevrolet with a soft top and it looked like a hearse. There was no such thing as a heater or an air conditioner but we were riding. When Daddy went to buy the car he got a driving lesson from the dealer (a driver's license was not required), and he set off bump-bump-bumping along. He continued the bump-bump-bumping all his life. When FAMC played Morris Brown in football that season he and Mother set off in the car to the game and stripped the gears on that red clay hill that led to FAMC. Guess who was left in charge at home.

After Daddy got the job teaching we had a lady to come on

Mondays to help with the wash. Soon thereafter, we took the clothes to her home on Sunday afternoon and picked them up on Monday or Tuesday afternoon.

The summer of 1935 brought changes to our surroundings. Daddy painted the church and our abode. Mother began working on the yard. We couldn't afford grass seed, but there was a profusion of St. Augustine grass in the ditch beside the grounds. We children were sent to pull up the grass in the ditch and replant it blade by blade in the yard. Mother also planted flowers in the space beside the church. The soil was rich and everything seemed to grow in profusion in Florida. After Mother took down the clothesline that our white neighbors had erected on church property, the whole place looked better.

St. Michael's began to thrive. Many of the former members returned, and a choir was organized. Mrs. Shirley tolerated that foot pedal organ, and there was a Sunday School made up of the four of us and a few others. The first confirmation class was in the spring of 1935. There were four or five confirmands. I remember one, me (I was nine years old). Bishop Juhann was our bishop. The children looked forward to his coming. He always told a bible story that was understood by the children as he developed his sermon.

I don't know Daddy's salary. As St. Michael's was a mission, the church paid an amount that was supplemented by the diocese. The whole thing was probably a hundred dollars a month or less. The school salary was probably less than a hundred. The missionary boxes continued to keep us well clothed.

There were Christmas programs and parties. A parish usually sent a box of Christmas toys and books for the tree. There were Easter egg hunts and cantatas. There was one cantata that we used at least twice in Tallahassee. All of us Gordons know "Easter Day." There was another song in it that I was to sing in duet with Ike Morris. (That name just jumped out of my memory). Mrs. Norwood, my piano teacher was helping to direct the program. Of course, I never could carry a tune. After much rehearsal, Mrs. Norwood told Mother, "Mrs. Gordon, she can't sing it." My Mother replied, "Well she is going to do it." And I did.

The car allowed us to drive out on Sunday afternoon to go to one of the small crystal lakes that dot Florida. We could watch the fish swimming. Or we could go to the white-owned store that Mother called the "Jim Crow" to get hamburgers, or even go to Thomasville, Georgia, just north of the Florida line to visit a fellow priest, Father Perry. The Perrys had several sons older than we were. They all went to St. Augustine's College. One was a Tuskegee fighter pilot during WWII. Another settled in Virginia Beach where he and his wife, also a St. Aug. alum directed the St. Aug Alumni Weekend until they died in the 1990s.

We also went to Quitman, Georgia to visit Daddy's sister, Teto; to Macon to visit Aunt Morsey, and to Forsythe to visit Mama Gordon. Quitman was a day trip but Macon and Forsythe were overnight trips.

The summer of 1936 took us to Sparta, GA, Mother's birthplace where Papa had built a little brick hovel on the land that Mama had bought years before with her egg money. Papa was very sick and he soon died at the age of 58 a few months before Michael was born. Michael was born Mother's color with straight hair. All of Mother's other children were born yellow. Of course Bobby and I soon turned black. Mrs. Baker claimed that the baby looked like her brother, Wyatt. So Michael was named Michael for St. Michael's Church, Vinzant for Daddy's head acolyte, Vinzant Pottsdamer, and Wyatt for Mrs. Baker's brother. Those namesakes became Michael's Godparents. So Michael Vinzant Wyatt Gordon was introduced to an already crowded house.

Christmas of 1935 we received a gift of a movie projector from Aunt Olive ("Sister") in Pittsburgh. We were the only third world people with a movie projector. We watched Mickey Mouse as Steamboat Willie over and over again. It never occurred to us to ask for another film. On another Christmas Sister sent us a beautiful, large, illustrated book of Hans Christian Andersen Fairy Tales. We were mesmerized by the stories. It was my job to read them to the boys before the 8 o'clock bedtime.

On hot summer nights we were allowed to stay up later until the house was cooler. We would look up at a huge starry sky that stretched infinitely far. Now and then we would see a "shooting star." We didn't know about meteorites entering the earth's atmosphere. We did know that the stars would disappear when there was a full moon. When we tired of gazing at the firmament we would catch lightening bugs and put them in a jar with a perforated top.

After that first hard-working summer we spent many summer days exploring. We scoured nearby woods and found plum trees, blackberries and sparkling lakes. The big experience that most of us remember was a trip to Panacea. There a bridge spanned an inlet of the Gulf of Mexico. People had been known to come back from fishing on that bridge with big red snappers that covered the top of the car. We weren't so lucky but all of us fished from the bridge. There were few cars crossing that bridge in the mid nineteen-thirties. The children were safe. We didn't feel so safe when somebody caught a stingray.

There were other outings. One was a church picnic on the Ochlocknee River. Men were hired to catch fish and have them ready to eat when the picnickers arrived. It was on these grounds that I saw sugar cane being ground by having a harnessed horse going around the mill. The family had a Memorial Day picnic on the grounds of the church that housed Daddy's school. We took our food and spread it on a blanket under a tree. This was much cooler than our crowded house.

We were in Tallahassee for four-and-a-half years. I went from age 8½ to 13. My memory is often not chronological, but I try.

I don't remember Daddy being ordained to the priesthood. I do remember being confirmed at age nine. I wore a white dress, a veil, white shoes and socks. I carried a bouquet of flowers for I was bride of the church. I never got to be so dressed again.

The Women's Auxiliary as it was called then became active. The first fund-raiser was a series of bingo parties in member yards beginning with the church yard. Lights were strung and the fun began. There were three or four of these before coming to an abrupt end. I don't know who objected, the Diocese or the city.

Then there were the Follies of 1930-something written and directed by Mother in the style of movies popular at that time. There was the young lady who craved stardom in New York played by Viva Spearman; her boyfriend played by Vinzant Pottsdammer and a cast of would-be stars played by Julian and Nat Adderley, Rawn Spearman and others. The auditorium at FAMC was booked, and tickets were sold. There was a mix-up on the dates, and the College didn't honor the agreed-upon date but made a settlement. It was fun while the cast rehearsed. They always practiced at our house. I don't remember any sets or any costumes and props for a Broadway Show. They were lucky that college made a mistake.

FAMC was a powerhouse at football in those days. As a part of the halftime show, Rawn would always toss the baton over the goalpost to count the number of touchdowns that the team had made by that time. The crowd would cheer each time he caught the baton.

I was considered for the lead in the operetta, "Cinderella" but I was not selected because I couldn't sing or dance. I was a daisy in a chorus:

> Daisies, daisies here today,
> From the meadow far away.
> All in line and dressed so fine
> With our daisy faces all a shine.

All of us daises were clad in green organdy dresses with ruffles. I was grown before I learned to wave my hand in time to the music while we went though our Daisy Paces. Our poor mother had to wait a long time before she had a child that had the looks and talents that she envisioned when she married that yellow man.

When I graduated from the sixth grade I attended school "up on the campus" at FAMC. Here we changed classes according to subject matter. The whole college began school when the bell was rung by hand in the quad in the center of the campus. We rushed to get to school on time. We would often beg the bell ringer to keep ringing until we entered our building. I enjoyed my classes and did well (I did have some talents) except in P E, which was sheer agony to me.

At home, I had much responsibility but no authority. The babies could hit me, but I couldn't hit them back. In the summer I did my share of the household chores. When we ironed, I had a board and Mother had one. When we made cakes for Sunday dinner, Mother made a cake and I made one. I did rise up when I was twelve and refuse to go to church. Mother said "O.K. but if you stay at home, you must cook dinner." It sounded like a winner to me. But, dinner was walking around in the yard. I killed the chicken, picked it, cleaned it, and cooked it. I also cooked string beans and made potato salad. I never refused to go to church again.

Some time after Michael was born in 1936, Mother went to work. She taught at a grade school in Leon County. She immediately subscribed to professional magazines, and went to summer school at FAMC as long as we were in Tallahassee.

I can't remember the caretakers of the children while Mother worked. Whoever she was must have kept the children at her home for I can't remember a person coming to our house. I do remember that she, after a time, refused to keep Ronald so

Mother had to take him to school with her.

By the time I was twelve we had made the home almost livable. The yard was neat and well kept. (Everything grows profusely in Florida). Mother and Daddy were both working; we were well fed and reasonably well dressed. We had a 1936 hard top Chevrolet for outings and trips. We had a good stove and a sink in the kitchen. We did not have a bath tub (except the ones used for washing clothes.)

It was a few days before Easter and the church children were practicing for the Easter cantata. Daddy was raking the front yard after cutting the grass. After practice, the children of the church ran over the church-yard and into the yard of our white neighbor, Mr. Luke next door. Mr. Luke came out and chased the kids. The words he used were not friendly. Daddy started toward Mr. Luke with the rake still in his hand. Mother followed Daddy saying, "Intelligent people don't settle arguments this way." The children were mesmerized. My brothers still think of this confrontation as Daddy's shining hour. The situation was diffused but Mother was scared. We moved the following week to a two-bedroom house behind the college campus. My bed was the living room studio couch. But, we had a bathroom.

We lived in that house for almost a year. Early in 1939 the bishop of the Diocese of Georgia called Daddy to repay the Diocese for his seminary training. Daddy was to supply St.

Stephen's Church in Savannah for the Lenten season and then report to St. Mary's Church in Augusta to serve for at least two years.

The church in Savannah was St. Stephen's on the east side. It had a large congregation, and a rectory that was large enough to accommodate us. It had big stuffy furniture. In those days people did not pay much attention to children's needs. Our school year was broken up so that we were in school in Savannah for about two months and then in Augusta for only a month before summer vacation. I don't remember being too unhappy about returning to Savannah. But the east side of Savannah where St. Stephen's was located was a lot different than the west side where we lived before. The church was in a busy area near the harbor. The battleship "Savannah" was docked there.

The boys were mesmerized by the city traffic. Remember Tallahassee was still a small town that didn't have public transportation. Savannah had street cars that passed just beyond our small backyard. The boys would yell, "Here comes the street-car. This one is a silver one." Soon a yellow one would pass and they let out a yell again. I was mortified.

I went to the public school in Savannah. I had gone to school at FAMC in Tallahassee and I was not prepared for the raucous public school that was Kyler-Beach High School. I remember an incident where the principal raised his hand in the auditorium to ask for order and somebody hit the hand with a spitball. I was in the ninth grade and had to take second semester Latin when I had not been exposed to Latin at all in Tallahassee. That was a crying time. The boys had their own problems. Walking home from school was another trial. I had a long walk through a white neighborhood to get home. The children there thought it was fun to throw rocks at me as I passed through. But it didn't last too long. After Easter, it was on to Augusta.

Augusta was a city also, but much smaller than Savannah. The church was a small white clapboard building. It was really rather pretty. It had no rectory, so we had to find accommodations which turned out to be a large house on 12th Street. Later we moved to a brand-new housing project, Sunset Homes. The opening was on the news reel in the movie theater, and all four of the boys were in the news.

I wasn't allowed to go anywhere without four brothers tagging along as chaperones. Daddy knew the man who managed the movie theater, and every time the boys wanted to go to the theater, they could get in for free by just telling the usher, "Rev. Gordon's children." I refused to go with them for free. Movies only cost a nickel in those days.

In Augusta, the streets were paved in front of the white people's houses, but not on our side of the street. Whenever there was a parade, we had to stand on our side, while the white people had a better view from the paved side. When George tried to go to the other side of the street, Bobby told him that only white people could go on the other side. George responded, "When I grow up, I'm going to be white."

I completed High School in Augusta at Payne College in 1941. When we moved to Charles Town in 1941, Mother was pregnant with Toni. She told me years later she was glad that she was pregnant when we arrived, because there were many young girls in Charles Town who were pregnant. If she had arrived with a baby, people might assume that Toni was my child.

We took the train from Augusta to Charles Town. The "Colored Section" of the train was up front directly behind the engine, so we got all the smoke. It was a long train that had to back into the station when we got to Washington, DC. There we changed to a small train with a big smokestack that went over many rivers and bridges to Harper's Ferry. The people from the church met us at the station and they had a big celebration in the Parish Hall for the new priest and his family. We thought they talked funny, saying things like, "Indeed, I do." We met Jimmy who said "Your house has a sister under it." It was a long time before we understood that he was saying *cistern*.

At first the rectory had 2 outhouses, one was for the church. When they installed indoor plumbing they connected the pipes wrong and the toilet flushed hot water. We still didn't have a bathtub, but rather took our baths in the kitchen in a big galvanized tub.

We made our own lye soap from pig fat that we got from the family next door who raised pigs. We had chickens, ducks, and guinea hens. Sometimes the chickens would stand on the fence and lay eggs so they would drop on the ground and break. We had two roosters that we called Big Boss and Little Boss. Big Boss was always trying to fight Little Boss until little Boss took him on, and killed him. That was the day we had Big Boss for dinner. Daddy showed us how to kill chickens by swinging them around by their head until their neck broke. Then the body would run around without the head. Mother did it a different way. She would hang the chickens on the clothes line by their feet, and then she would cut their heads off. That way, she didn't get blood all over the place, and the chicken didn't run around. In the spring, the boys bought biddies, which they put in a box with a light bulb to keep them warm.

I attended college at Storer College in Harper's Ferry until Daddy arranged for me to enroll in St. Augustine's College in Raleigh. After Toni was born, Mother tried to get a job teaching, but there were no jobs in Charles Town. When she learned of jobs in Washington, DC, she went there to work at the Navy Annex during the week, and came home to Charles Town on the weekends. Mother enjoyed her work there in Washington, but she didn't like having to ride in the back of the bus.

I was at St. Augustine's when the family moved to Petersburg, but they told me of the adventure they had packing and moving. They were packing a trunk downstairs when Mother sent George upstairs to find the trunk in the attic. George stepped between the rafters, and fell through the ceiling, landing in the trunk downstairs. That trunk closed, "WHAM" with George inside. When everybody started calling, "Where's George," he popped up out of the trunk all covered with dust, and said, "Here I am," as if by magic.

Daddy had a big moving truck to take them, and the driver started out in the wrong direction, heading to Petersburg, West Virginia by mistake. When they arrived in Petersburg, they were amazed by the big church tower on St. Stephen's Church, but Bobby told them "Don't look up or people will think we're from the country." They walked all over town looking at the tall (4-story) buildings. Somebody warned them not to walk on the wrong side of the street, but the boys didn't pay any attention and nobody stopped them.

I was sixteen when I arrived at St. Augustine's College in Raleigh. I started out majoring in Chemistry, but changed to Mathematics. It was the first time in my life that I had a room all to myself, and a real bed. My room was a closet in the dormitory room that I shared with two other girls. I had a scholarship to cover my tuition, but I had to work. My first job was washing and ironing clothes in the school laundry. Soon after I started hearing students in the dining hall complaining that somebody had messed up their shirts, my job was changed to the library. Miss Snodgrass was the librarian who also taught Bible. She would get so caught up in the Scripture that she would say things like, "I just loved Peter." Miss Snodgrass became my mentor and directed me to do the right things as an Episcopalian. She even wanted me to go into a convent. When I told Mother, she said, "No you won't be going there." It was Miss Snodgrass that had us girls to scrub the steps to the chancel in St. Augustine's Chapel. I stayed in touch with Miss Snodgrass for years after I left St. Aug.

When I graduated from St. Aug in 1945, Mother was pregnant with Sarah. Pregnant women weren't seen at public events in those days, so Mother didn't attend my graduation. My classmates nicknamed Sarah before she was born as "Who Woulda Thought It." After graduation I took my first job near Charlotte, NC teaching math and science at Plato Price High School. I stayed there one year before moving on to the next chapter of my life.

Post Script

Well, Family,

That was LaVerne's story, with some of the facts from Charles Town provided by George. To quote LaVerne, "Our poor mother had to wait a long time before she had a child that had the looks and talents that she envisioned when she married that yellow man." I don't know who LaVerne meant by that statement. You will have to read my memoir coming soon, <u>Motherless Child, stories from a life</u>, to decide if I fit that vision. I hope the rest of you will be inspired to complete your own stories before they are lost.

S.G.W.

www.ingramcontent.com/pod-product-compliance
Lightning Source LLC
Chambersburg PA
CBHW031331040426

42443CB00005B/296